RAVAGE & SNARE

RAVAGE & SNARE

POEMS

Matthew Carey Salyer

Pen & Anvil Press
BOSTON

Copyright © 2019 by Matthew Carey Salyer
All rights reserved
Published in the United States

ISBN 978-0-9916222-9-0

Permissions inquiries:
Pen & Anvil Press
P.O. Box 15274
Boston Mass. 02215
www.penandanvil.com

Designed by Zachary Bos
Set in Minion Pro, with titling and
details in Dalle and Silverfake

A note on the layout: Some recto pages bear
a chain ornament in the footer, to indicate
the continuation of text onto the verso.

for Meghan Maguire Dahn

Table of Contents

I. Letters to a Noble Lord

12	Reliques of the Great Immigrant Songbook
13	Anaconda American Brass
14	All the Youngbloods
14	The Electoral History of the Carey Family
17	Do-Right Man
18	Behold, Be Held
20	Fam, Innit
21	Catholic Boy
22	Either, or Us
24	Copland
26	Hunter, Hemographer
27	Department of Social Services
30	Silly Old Bear
32	Letters of the Absentee
33	Singlehanded
34	Recasting Self-Portrait as the MTA Lost Property Office
36	Watching the Fights at The Tryon House While Lorca Says *Duende*

II. A Vindication of Natural Society

40	Hudson Line
41	How You Were Got
42	Myself as a Foreign Country
43	After Watching *Mad Max*
44	Coney Island Girl
46	You Ask to Buy a Gun from Me in Aux Cayes
47	The Boy in the British Museum
48	Some Do
49	Sandpiper
50	Tweeting Aleppo
51	The Children of Lir

52	Bewailes Me
53	A Record of Some American Officers in the Egyptian Army of Isma'il Pacha After Appomattox
54	A New York State Trooper Explores the Link Between Arrowhead Hunting and Methamphetamine Withdrawal
55	Everything Is Permitted
56	New York City Placement Exam
61	Cocaine as *Trompe L'œil* of the Beatific Vision in the Upper East Side
62	I Regret One of Nine Tattoos Below the Elbow That Violate the Proper Appearance and Wear of My Uniform in Accordance with AR-670-1

III. Conciliation with America

66	Argonaut
67	Arse Poetica
68	Lords of Inwood
69	The Cloisters
70	My Father Reading *The Sound and the Fury*
72	Brooklyn in Postcards of Soviet Russian Fairy-Tales
74	Key War in A Minor
75	Ask the Birds
77	Northern Passage
78	Our Late Departure
81	Before Marriage
82	Virgil Explains Limbo to Dante
83	Incomplete Self-Portrait as the Last Words of Saints
85	Wild Colonial Boy
87	*Notes & Sources*

*Pigeons were the first loving relationship
I ever had. As a matter of fact, when a bully
that was antagonizing me killed one of my birds
in front of me, I snapped and began fighting him.*
– Mike Tyson

After a revolution, all events seem pale.
– John Crowe Ransom

I

LETTERS TO A NOBLE LORD

It's Lambkin was a mason gude
As ever built wi stane;
And built Lord Wearie's castle,
But payment got he none.

– Child Ballads 93.A

Reliques of the Great Immigrant Songbook

Reader, even the NYPD Choir will go back
to work when their usefulness ends. Run faster,

if you like. For each year here, stripe yourself once
like sheepshead. Unfold, from the claw of my ribs,

my due heart into this phantom republic of mouths.
Be patient, Lady Zero. All that is in me and able

brakes against transfigurations for the Public Good.
I have interrupted the policed conversation of trees

to bend your ear like a shivering seat for the hart
I am in this conceit, pleading its deadfall:

authentic turnings of my family's great fable,
unhunted in salt-licking season, this fine feeding.

Anaconda American Brass

In the last hour I have been cowering
under the tremendous radium of the evening
before I left home, the grim brick dray
of the riversides, the be-all.

How many moments scanned in a faraway
until the machine shop smokestacks,
the shining breath of their scarves, stopped,
down to the cellars, the dry sockets

under your cure, where I was wondering why.

All the Youngbloods

after an epigram of St. Thomas More

I think you're expecting meaning to belabor –
where the sick fox caverns, the lion ties its wreath,

he said; he said he'd lick the lion, not the lion's teeth.
So do good neighbors, meaning no harm, keep us

just beyond arm's reach, safe as the feed the barn
dog guards because it wants to eat the horse.

In all this extravagance, more like life's haphazard
course and happenstance than the plan of epigrams,

this life unlike heaven for having, the dog and the horse
in the barn and the house with the face in the window

are always you – in it all, isn't all real paradox
about pain in that it resembles our neighbors?

In that, it resembles our neighbors who killed the fox
with the dog the barn horse killed to get the feed

and the nothing we saw and the never we lions breed.

The Electoral History of the Carey Family

Lord Rift, remember to our blue heaven, how
the sound of my grandfather's prime was a suite
    of pink mice in the elephant field
        tobacco he worked, and echoes his step-
            mother tucked

under his wag tongue from *An tImleach Mór*. Meet
the Careys in a dollhouse diorama
    of unexplained death they've made my head
        house: mouse-mother, mouse-father, ratkin to
            amuse, me.

In the house-head, my hand trimmed down their thimble
town to a crime scene for fam. Silence, its great
    custody. Move manmade miniature
        us through whitewash autumn, 1960,
            when we could

not yet be faulted for what work does, for Jack
Kennedy said that we had 'the easiest
    city or else the best Democrats
        in the damn state.' How's gone wrong? Rush, ratkin.
            This is just

experimental architecture for ghosts
two decades before I was born lost, host, full
    stop. So all year long I've been looking
        for affordable housing in the blue,
            good districts

on an electoral map of the Tristate,
like trying to find cause for an accident
    in a lab where rats in mazes ran
        hot then cold with some rare incurable
            disease. Please

do not touch the dollhouse ethnographic scene.
The Unclaimed Death of the Carey Family
    takes only the slightest disturbance
        to be like the last hurrah, be like just
            fucking touch me.

Do-Right Man

North mill towns so big so hard to die however did.
My ma still pensions their parliament of graves and I do
the right thing. I'm told I fit, strong face, keep fit, but class
is bone-bred, guess. So put me to bed, bet you
bounce. I'll do the right thing and you do you,
you know? For the scene I flip the script, picture
me back on the block as a mode of time travel, theatrics
of Tennyson's Camelot, that mashup meant to metric
heaven, *therefore never built at all and therefore built
forever,* from which the knight sets forth, the hero
my kid believes I am at turns and O I swear I do
turn. Equally possible: her love, how the wool light
draws over Hudson heaven, blank as Mordred's shield,
and night means *naught,* not *dead.* I populate it
with Breughel's version of *The Man Who Fell to Earth*
when she denies I loved her mother like a little
sister and I dream I am the description
of rare old times, a mill town upriver, left
nosebleed corner on the Master's canvas, safe berth.
But what's with the galleons, slipping like wooden shoes
from some subliminal goal, no crew to care? And annulment.
That. Ask the wax man washing himself of his wings
or the lawnmen, pacing their dull incisions in foreshore,
who bow their heads to the rut and do-right, do-right.

Behold, Be Held

On First Reading Wordsworth's "My Heart Leaps Up
When I Behold" on the Bx7

With heather dusk, who'd sent his cuckoo

    to the rainbow ward pounded a noon

        prism to mere word;

    who'd found, two shits

for shacktown, moral ordinates for speech

    in a limewashed homeplace,

        sounded crooks

of lake between the bluff's toes:

    he beheld and said 'beheld.'

Other, I hold to garish in preludes of Bronx,

    thinking that time

        unwraps in the cerement grass

until 'the child is father to the man' –

    remind me, now, of all those goodwill saviors at school

        who preached 'plain living,

            but high thinking,' not thinking

common men, in great

       'spontaneous overflows of passionate feeling,'

will take your head straight off.

How untouchable and closed

    I find the heart is, made

        to perform the innocence of others,

           for others,

        unopposed,

but now, when the masters of this art

        come for the man in me,

           here,

or here,

    where I have made the generations

        I am their grace,

I will know how quiet

        he must be, held

until they have spoken, until I have broken

        all of my bones in their embrace.

Fam, Innit

I can't tell you why I imagine the shoal because
I do. I've tried thinking it's more picturesque
than picaresque, like those old pricks in the tidy
town: Michael the Ferry because he ran the boat
to Portmagee, my grandfather's cronies with cases
of salmon from somewhere means somewhere, done.
We've still a good back in the country, now back
at the local bolloxed, prawn on brown loaf for lunch,
a generation since uncles. Here's ma with a half-
pint, half-expecting they'll tromp in, all broth,
cigarettes flicked like weathercocks, black suits
and those rubber fisherman boots. Cheers, the time
Michael took the taken salmon crates and sold them back
to the right Proprietors & Sons, no bones
about it. The cats of a kind in a loop of cahoots.
Then there was after the time my grandma said Uncle
Brian had taken a job in China when everyone knew
he was doing an eight-year stretch in the pen.
Next time I saw him, we walked on people's hands
outside Grauman's Chinese Theater and he said *look,
you know what this is? Just someone's bullshit – all
this was once an idea.* I imagine the shoal
sands covered with salmon because I have an idea
that choking must feel like all our calamitous mistakes,
because I see the uncles raking in seal weather, beaten
like hard stumps, and I dig them by the black of my nails.

Catholic Boy

> *I put my tongue to the rail whenever I can*
> *– Jim Carroll*

Prots, picture my picture-book saint, posed
for baroque life studies, casket on catafalque,

as the Conqueror Worm evacuates his architecture
like a child's rumor of god:
                      uprising, unveiling: affirm

this theatre, Flesh, that brooks no metaphor in lineaments
of this world. Make 'soul' its substitute pearl

for which he dove beneath a lambent page of sea
in literal demonstration of his Word.

Should you suppose what self-composure must be
required to conspire with children in their close

proximity to such obscene delights, it might explain
my boredom with the *coup de grâce*

in this church where no celebrant scuttles, disrobes
a monstrance, pries the carapace, and tries to lurch forth

                our dogma of trilobites quivering brawn.

Either, or Us

Comes the fear our ma goes next, a sole
required handmaid to our father the lore:

North and wraith, all that foxfire.
For forfeiture, I'll listen to you thump

your great orations on my cheek turned,
lecterned, hairless as a first communicant,

to be the knocking at the gate in *Macbeth*.
I have lived in this jar the years of you

as nodding king, enthroned, matted in idiot
pelt below a mace of head. Ours, either.

Come dreams, our father's buried here,
shrunk to this Great Hall, my one-and-heir,

and long since I built the casket scaled to flea,
placed him within it, uttered inaudible

jeweler's-locket requiems, the porters
(poor beetles at the turning key) report

the exterior world's become a masterpiece
of confusion – they have held my tongue

like a fat adder, its numb screw rooted
for the doubled *grave, matter,* but now

you bring armies of wood razed to wicker men
and obscure brutes clamor the livelong.

Come at me brother.
Let us see who stole whose blood from whom.

Tomorrow is knocking out my teeth from within.

Copland

This ingathered year, not all able outwore
the habits of love, for which old things occur.
Winter, their mandible. Muzzled,

I sweat to critter, creasing
the moon in its envelope of sheets, unsure
of whom to hubbub or halve –

who, you, clever, clearer?
For what. Words, worlds, both; both
bleak as erudite, conjecture their phantom

iterations of the chronotope when
I open the note of my bed for the nether
lives in mine. Take unconsciousness.

It rubs like grit under a nacre of wet pelt,
directing the speculative creatures to proper
traps in which odd things concur –

edge of a city furnished with white month,
its pewed streets wedged in a map craw
of hill for parochial dead, precedent

as anticipation, the aural geographies
of church-bells and craic, brown-paper
errands, bars phrased for our dear terrorists,

and grandma's ache washing my bloody mouth
in a dispersal of many tongues

I lied with after kingmaking fights at school.

I tune in that same obedient silence as you
say you'd never love me in the NYPD.
I have never become a good liar, a new man,

but what I meant was something about the neighbor's
pit that bays like a neighbor at freewheeling day,
something about such joy as when we met restrained.

Hunter, Hemographer

I am a man scrubbing clean on a knife.
I am a dog with a tonsure.

The accomplishments of others are unreal.
Children are unreal

at this distance, and this
provides some consolation for their slight

to the work of work.
Come, judged, little strangers, to judge

my stranger disbelief in you.
I count ten tines from the brow, but milk teeth.

Tell me the wonders of unfinished things
and I will finish the blood land.

Department of Social Services

Here, last hymn's "The Norman Conquest,"
    composed by ten Ms. Joneses from DSS
        whose one name's impressed
        on business cards
    clipped to polling questionnaires for the Great Hearths,
a Lord Exchequer's pastoral

unclouded like the infringement of hawks –
    Do x-number hounds unscrew from the burrows?
        Where do x hares flick oaks'
        great nerves from within
    like restless thoughts? Go on, put down your pencils,
Ms. Joneses, throw me a bone, go home,

stop checking my refrigerator,
    talking to old neighbors, asking for receipts.
        Ms. Joneses, I know
        you're sick of being
    part of the outer-borough illuminati.
Put down your clipboards, hike up your dull goose

skirts, and have, as you say, a bless'd day.
    It's true I've put down your flat-heel Payless shoes
        in our interviews
        but I hanker, hot
    at the thought of asking you to take them off
because something beautiful inclines

from our inmost to what you think blessed
    defines, an 'obliviousness in delight,'
        from the Old English

>   blīths (bliss) not blētsian,
>   (blessing) which pulls from the root word blōd, for blood
> consecrating real things to uses, for good.
>
> Last Doomsday, while you were counting kings,
>   I redevised the unicorn cloven,
>   more goat than longhorn
>   virgin, its virtues
>   engendered for use. In fairness, I'm just
> a man accustomed to excise as the form
>
> incited by most revelations
>   of the inner life. I, too, could count myself
>   king if one damn thing
>   after another
>   came to mind so suiting my preoccupations
> to realities, made my lot whole.
>
> Ms. Joneses, I'd fuck you uselessly all
>   at once in the Dept. of Social Services
>   where I see myself
>   without the talking
>   cure for outside voices outworn like old shoes –
> take Hannah Arendt, who called family men
>
> 'this century's grand adventurers'
>   last century, its compromised conspirators
>   who make their poem
>   paterfamilias
>   and are thus the condemned verbs of revisions.
> 'It must feel the same on any scale,'

I said, 'to have known the day's blessing
    receding like bliss, like preoccupations
        with those whom you loved
          obliviously.'
    You never know how to reply, Ms. Joneses.
I'm unambitious but I know my own

blood, sitting on this diecast office chair
    with the red plastic seat, awkward as medieval
        kings illustrating
          one damn thing after
    its use in Holinshed's Chronicles
of England, Scotland, and Ireland:

    'Tell me more of the law,' quod Richard, Coeur-de-Lion
    in anno domini 1189, 'and how the king is a poet.'

'Not even an ox, nor cow, nor goat,
    was there that was not set down,' quod the catspaw
        Ms. Joneses, 'thank God.
        And that's why we called
    the book Domesday: because it is, like the day
of the Last Judgment, unalterable.'

'Then show me the list,' the Lion, 'and where it says why.'

Silly Old Bear

Girlhood takes practice, like all proper violence.
Perhaps that's why I find it so natural
to accommodate the work

of my daughters: their princess rehearsals, doll covens,
and the confusing menagerie of picture-book
killers with animal families.

There are never any mothers in their wild,
just the spontaneous generation of carnivore males'
cubs, and I, poor naturalist that I am,

must be constantly reminded of this fact; I must be shown
slovenly cats, bachelor wolves, bruised bad bucks,
and the silly old bear – they are all a mess

of me. Consider this, then: what makes Owl coax a suicide
of drones from my fur, or Rabbit unlock the queen's comb
from my craw? It isn't love, it's fear. Not much

use telling that to daughters, though. Children are medievalists,
sucking crucifixion through every broken reed
in the Hundred-Acre Wood,

and allegorizing every cub lost to the teat. Let them.
Girlhood looks so arduous, and it must feel good
to keep a killer beside you,

buttoned in bearskin. Who else should raise daughters?
Who else can make a hunter like a hunter?

I work the work my wild things pursue:

What did you think I was doing all these years?

My paws clang in a bother of brown pots and honey.
Didja hear me coming? Didja-didja?
We could scare me to death.

Letters of the Absentee

after Jean-Elmouhoub Amrouche

Tanglefoot in the roots
of a wet star,

unhand
the secret mass of birds,
their core

of honey and sand,
to the inner world where I am
griever and God.

Singlehanded

Black apertures in a field of ghost,
they come to me when the winter will be
their last, tacked in weather and slick cinch.

When we collapse, we collapse by the common law
of us. I do not peel the foil of cold from our stupor.
I forget the lame hocks, fine as you'd guess,

and my jaw shovels a hum from the animal lung
I face. If it were so easy to throw a horse down,
you would all do it, you would hold

their tantrums with a strap.
No one can tell me how bold and lonesome
sires choose their falls or me,

but I throw horses.
What a burden, what a beast
I've been.

Recasting Self-Portrait as the MTA Lost Property Office

False destinies, son. No love for the 7
    train crowd, their density. Hygge, hygge, O my
        master's partner's
    children from her previous life.
Lords Convenient, your children will lose your shit
    in their social apparatus
    for quick minds:
    train-talk, bud, Tinder, twaddle. But
underground, in the phantomic station ogives, once,
    behind bricks: trust:

I was a true detective. I can tell you
    there are lots of honest people
        in Manhattan
    with few hang-ups, run-of the-mills
who'll take time to bring iPhones & Kindles
    to the MTA Lost Property Office
        at Penn Station,
    its ellipsis in the lower
level's wall where strangers fill in parts of themselves
    through description

beneath the organized movement of workers
    exiting trains, the sound of trains, sound of the
        world letting go
    of small polylingual ballast
before reentering its trajectories
    upward into kinesthetic
        darkness. Feint, heart,
    complete your moon landing. Because

I could not hold the complex original
        of myself well,

I have been coming here from #WoodlawnTheBronx
        to acquire replacement parts
                from the Office:
        new glasses, misericord knees, heart
defibrillators, rock shandies, umbrellas,
        social security numbers,
                Richard's cork leg.
        This new Matthew Carey Salyer
will look less the stairwell rat, tah-dah, will lumber
                less, and all that

I want to remember about the Great House
        will sprout like vines from this new tongue,
                this corbel nose
        that bears an old brow on black eyes
where I have not yet placed the wafer of moonrise
        to see me with an iron chest,
                this broadchurch bell
        in which I will everyday wake…
Do you see, Lady Zero? My mother's house has left you
        a man for sons.

Watching the Fights at The Tryon House While Lorca Says Duende

Like Iron Mike,
I would bring my lips to your ear and eat

your children praise be because like Mike
lived juvie, I'm fatherless, foundered like iron in gloves

on soft spots.

Like his sweet-bellied
birds, I would be something I could be

a fool for,
your living blue note.

II

A VINDICATION OF NATURAL SOCIETY

'O pay me, Lord Wearie,
Come pay me out of hand:'
'I canna pay you, Lambkin,
Unless I sell off my land.'

– Child Ballads 93.A

Hudson Line

Hobbesian, hiving, we clutched the borough's hem
in blear, implacable as children, as leviathan

estuaries, furrowed with scull, strove like one
mind's variance with itself. Their spit whorled breath

on the station's iron crown, spun its reel of solved
phantoms in panorama: corporate, incorporate,

The Commuter is always facing the wrong way
when the northbound comes to fatten its silver bone.

I have come to regard him as the evolution of species,
all the different men I might have become

with entitlement, grace, fearing most things he must do
alone, while replacement crowds, roosting on scarp,

gawk crewed hulls, rowers fixing each rib
to the costume sternum, hearts in half-life; mud,

armored in smooth stones, clambers our strand
from fountainhead, drying its face on roots

until it's our own, an afterlife of grit on rails and game
to hear my voices shuttle through the hissing reeds –

but what good is loneliness if we must share it?

        Whose voice, when I call you, runs late?

How You Were Got

Once was a landscape resembling
white tarps, huffed on a purlin,
and I was the bullock with seven kills

waiting. I horned love sharp for your time.
Midwives kept you crowned in a hillock,
but you, braver than salmon, scuffled

to breathe in our Zion of jaundice and tar.
Then I clung to a landscape of seven kills
waiting, piercing a heaven by hand with horns

to call you, green and god-saved king, to tear
your ribbon from the mother's bone
that held you from this crying miracle of air.

Myself as a Foreign Country

after Anna Greki

The earth sleeps in the open and in my head
I'm still, my thoughts bare as the rigorous scrub

where swamp swaps its swept dross for breakers,
their clap snatching the tufted shore from behind

my emporium ear: all of my atoms seeds
that occlude this bloodrunning world, its tenderness:

all I have thought of this world resembling men
in amniotic vigor, falling into the public domain.

After Watching Mad Max

Missing the point of the pale
horse and star-striking bestiaries of God,
we end the epic of our dialectic
abandoned at intermission.
Hereafter, to covenant with prodigals,
to have foreclosed, in names, bones,
to have washed the warden's children
in petrol with connivance
until a village unhands their ash
to the leather men, hereafter
all this will mean is that you, revolving
on a spectacular gibbet
will have bet on the wrong
horse, history, on the wrong
in us. Come, driver, bring
twelve gauges of your anointing
as I thrash on the hanging thorn of a tree.

Coney Island Girl

I recall the machine
        of summer dazing salt
until I almost am. I think
        you were nine and green
for almost orphan then.
        A storm had buried its famous rage
in the longshore, lacking
        conventional forms of pity
though it had a human name.
        The aquarium was closed.

At the end of the world,
        we ate grease on kitsch
beach. See the Wonder Wheel
        because it says it is.
A man walked on images
        of water the glass chips made
supple as fire, and fire.
        The sideshow ran and got us:
God, the sword-swallower
        must have asked for a volunteer
from the crowd as I ignored you,
        thinking my father

could have been a circus
        strongman or boardwalk huckster
who'd swallow all the bills
        before his disappearing act: you,
realizing what you'd committed
        yourself to, asked me

what would happen
        if your hand slipped with the blade.
I told you everything
        that I have seen in this life
is afraid of an encore, a *tableau*
        vivant of interior pain
where the old men are
        burying hatchets,
still, raising Cain.

You Ask to Buy a Gun from Me in Aux Cayes

It's like grooming distance with a comb
across an earshot of room I borrowed from the family

background of all my harmless creditors
who speak at the archival pace of lice in your nap

about humanitarian crises, as though fear's nothing
but the managed population of natural syndromes

rewilding or diplomatic status for the hundred men
who matter in the underworld. First

one dreads this close acquaintance with homicides,
their hair-plumed helms on shadow-wired cheeks

however few in special Hades. Who among them
lords me over your boll earth, skewbald

with freehold, as fruit warts in the green fledge, a tetanus
of chattel for old debts, the vice-governor's mouthful?

For lesson, I'm lesion on an ass
being led to death in postcolonial illustrations for the gospel

I found in the Great Archive of the City, the one that falls
in all my dreams, between the last two books I'll read to the fire –

Kings, Nations –
until our last first breath, the death of death.

The Boy in the British Museum

Catalogued – a child and a child's
coffin cut to calculi of faces grieving
for a form. Perhaps this explains the custom
of carving these stupid sarcophagi with lost races,
leaving stock-still pennants and dolphin lap-
markers rough, the cupids half-relieved, the rock
rock. The metaphor's the self as charioteer,
overthrown too quickly by the race of life,
but I scan for the bereaved, a husband or wife
among the cherub crowds, my vital detail.
Where their claw-chisel kiddos drag the coarse
grain of undone laps, I see them in a lone
horse when it gags back, buck-wild in bridle.

Some Do

Check me on fleek like the night
kitchen mothers, pucker and hum some; come,
I like to liquor louche; let's watch the flock
of spring-heeled bound as borough cabs
exhaust their carbon phantoms like a gauche
of fuck. Do you unzoo, unrouged
to rat as white, what roughshod? Do.
I want the carnal as straight metacognition,
our sexes bundled like the primitive hardwire
of teleological automata,
arguing my provenance against
the famous world of time: prime
the nether, knee-jerk genuflections, grind
the gear-work, make you wonder whether
I could watch you like a kingdom come.

Sandpiper

Hell, here's me: don't know   the word for *sand*
is *sin*. I begin   with *The Woman in the Dunes*
as Parent's Day at West Point,   seeing an infant
footprint on my blackboard: soon, it's wiped away
my lecture notes on *Algérie   française*, first-hand
accounts of Aussaresses' death   squads, *Pied-Noir* farms
used to stage insurgent   suicides. Same, same.
Implied is that you can't   erase an erasure, only
what was meant, what was past   an edge of presence. Whatever
became of *the fragments of   feet in the slippers*
of young dancers found   at the bombing at Casino Cornice,
or the unverified account   of one legionnaire's fleet encounter
with a flying saucer in 1958,   *how it was like time
running very slowly*   without restraint, are also sand
on casing brass spun in the rifle   bore that flowers
across a topographical map   showing the past
has no escape route through   the earliest usage of *sand*
under the margin of my hand   in the coroner of my eye.

Tweeting Aleppo

Look: confused, like a busted bee dismounting its wall
from the brood frame's quarantine, its broken archive

a stick-smacked spill of production time, I want
you to picture a father in the black-and-white kill

zone of a hundred characters, your six legs in sand,
his serif of limbs, lines of the bombed blocks graphed

at different heights, the world as worn, and what
is a father then but part of the theory that drones can't see

the color red on a best dress and dear-heart,
of the sun's bloody head kicked by beasts of success?

The Children of Lir

Howbeit this brief counterfactual casts you
as swans: among nine green billows, sawn

from the shoal-work of black craft in rose
weather, you're climate. I'm astrolabe.

In love I lie lighthearted as life minds
our fetch of storm beach, its crest-fallen karst

sown with hairstreak and mink, the fuck-me
hoverflies a household of human forms

I will not concede: when you eavesdrop
my death as from 300 years of flight

and rowans ensnare you in their fluxing hair,
be restored to me in the secular sense.

Pray for us now & that hour the dust
stirs our framework of accurate names.

Bewailes Me

When you're done rehearsing dominion on doves,
do not be unstrung by all the white hoods

cast off in a laundry of wings, or aghast at the skulls,
unzipped, for which breakfast spins on a crib,

a chewable mobile of lower orders, turned on tong
noses like the antique plague doctor's mask.

The birds were never our mendicants.

No, nowhere is such a kingdom as heaven and no
fowl covenants with the humane, the iterative love

of poets for poets in its arboreal masques.
If you'd love a stranger, you must lend a hand

until you cannot get much closer to the ground.
You must humble yourself to the barbarous doves.

All the best tyrants have this command of the fauna,
the Jacobean personalities of crows. All rise, for God's

sake, flap.

A Record of Some American Officers in the Egyptian Army of Isma'il Pacha After Appomattox

Bespoke to first-blood like brides, your brevet sirs,
having made our civil union from divorced
themes, quit this undivided house for a laughing place.

Most, re-fielding the draught's yoke, let crop
rows balk in lark-hanging
quiet; others gun-slung a migrant largesse

on herd-sufficient plains. But ones I track
inflamed handsomeness the distance of mirrors:
Khartoum, far as the Horn, their too-composed abandon

farced the pleasure domes. For moral, think:
the Orient is the stage on which the whole East is confined,
then augment, *a theatrical stage affixed to Europe.*

Pretend this explains why the dustcoat gentlemen jilted
our virgin nation for a butcher's grace.
Do, or continue their flight in the bulrushes

as the river heaves its tramp of ceremonials,
all that hierophant. The secret's the sun is boring
under my raw hide, speculum of an ape.

No one bides homestead, quotidian, the masculine form
of despair, not when even lovers need to eat
themselves. Think: how thick is the membrane of thou.

A New York State Trooper Explores the Link Between Arrowhead Hunting & Methamphetamine Withdrawal

What's-a-body-to-do, you with your kickshaw
and me with you, is a tropic of accidents

run clean through grist village,
what's left – but right, right,

if you'd still opt for picture-perfect hills
jammed with A.M. stations, talking

hunting season, square light
floats in turret windows of the baronet

mansions like spinsters drinking cups of fireflies
live there. But who'd ever

leave the plump chrome diner and full-service
station for shiver pines, for drive-by

lacunae. Slow shift I home
an owl to watch the night work happen:

sometimes a grovel of tweakers
walking on mole hands, pull flint teeth

from a hairy jawline of ridge. Right
now, you could see how beautiful they do.

Everything Is Permitted

> *Shall we pick some flowers, Doctor?*
> *– Captain Kirk*

Rapt to the rock planet, I was dying
to see the outcome, the death I never did
understand, at least not clearly at all
of ten. The first episode's "The Man Trap."
To recap, the three leads appear on the moor.
Ruins, as in Canaan. The glade, the naked
ball-root flowers, sized like remorse
and aren't we all born to it, burdensome?
Here, on the colonial horizon, the heath
woman's creature-of-the-week, all glam.
Two go down and fine, I'm in love: the camphor
loneliness burns between the darling stars
is us. She is everything I ever wanted and to her
I am tall salt. When she falls, the leads talk
as though they've killed the last bison. Three
in the lazy evening. We four without fault.

New York City Placement Exam

Been done to death, Lord Spiritual, the holy
      'Hallelujah,' yeah? Thought its broken
           bone of a chord stuck where I cache harsh
upbringing thoughts in the throat (hush), *heave*:
      haw by haw I oust out wit, rage. Ow. Opt not.
         Hundredfold, the face-plant lambs
of the Northwest/South Bronx Region Catholic Schools
      would be grieving for want of a nail
in fresh-pressed, be 'bye, bish,' be 'said-you-said
      catch me outside.' We brat, we brute, worst rudi-
        ment. Boy, you schoolyard
      that flock and come correct at the punk hour,
when all we fight to want, our eyes our anthracite
      for the piece of work we are,
         dints us where hearts fickle

the complex lives of animals. It's too late. Fly-
      catcher, next time pick more baroque instruments
         than us. Ram I am I know but you
should wear the bell in this iteration. I'd die
      to lead you to sacrifice on our class trip
         at Lincoln Center thinking
not even the beautiful days, not one
      of the bird's-eye views of the earth
shares the smooth curve of the aneurysm
      that killed my dad, only the Met's opera-house
         ceiling, its great gilt
      meant to depict mad lives of the stars
at the explosive beginning of night
      bent on the orchestra pit.
         Cue incidental

music from an ensemble of john does for whom
        nothing ever prospered (and they know it). Said
                nope, kids from around-the-way with rare
minds are just regular guys born with tails. I hoped
        I could cut mine off. Lords Spiritual,
                the lesson I take away
from *The Death of King Saul According to God*
        (where everyone's damned like Horace Mann)
is that we can't all be royals, can we?
        The opera's first act depicts your wonderworking
                in the brief, freaky
        lives of kingdoms, the portrayed country-
side a sweep of green sanction for ambition.
        Almost all of the boys from school
                get into Fordham Prep

so we can perform most of the supporting roles
        as Lords Temporal and Lords Spiritual
                of the Cross-Bronx Expressway. CUNY's
a good school. Fordham's Jesuit, our taste of was.
        Your forefinger of plot pulls like a dog.
                I hawk the parallel graves
built for king-fathers from Row K, Seat 109.
        Fine dumb sons. O screw the grandeur. O what –
this is merit-based? Super. Cue my queue…
        Rex?… Rex?… next. His anointing was a roof of birds
                flown off with the self-
        righteous aloofness of his suicide.
Saul would never have said that he asked to be king.
        My dad only went to college
                to cry wolf one more time
in a basket of grass where lambs relive the birds'

        flight in the small throat of their shade. When you
            walk out of the Southern District of New York
federal prosecutor's office
        a free man, maybe you will see the worth
            of a good education…
like me, my dead dad've winked. That's one way to work
        for other people. Like children,
            our bodies outgrow us.

You will have one hour to finish the exam,
        the prophet warns the king in the final act.
            Question one. Do the yes-ma'ams moth me
after third period because I talk back smack?
        Fact. Matt is a capable student when he
            chooses to answer. Question
two. What are The Berkshires and how do you do
        you? The little legislators
on the Yearbook Committee require
        an about-me blurb asap. Funny's okay
            but look (no *you* look)
        keep it clean, upbeat. It's for your mother.
Fuckers, my mother got hit on by Michael Caine
        c. *Get Carter*, and my girl
            says that would explain

a world but the dates. Ma doesn't faze. Three. Great question.
        I think the first time was when the School Council
            demanded cans and contributions
for the down-and-out. Ha. Governor Cuomo
        visited our homeroom like a cardinal-
            archbishop, lest we get notions
nothing's changed under the new management.

        But there's a permanent record
on everyone. Bronx Science won't take me
        (the Lords of Discipline said) because they've heard
            'what he's really like'
from some good people with fat white teeth.
You have ten minutes left for the exam (breathe).
        Super. Senator Schumer,
            I am addressing

the optional essay portion of this exam
        to contributing listeners of WNYC,
            shy Tourists of the Charitable,
polishing handout cans, counting demands, c/o yourself.
        I have been learning to talk about myself
            by reading all of (what else?)
Richard Howard's poetic monologues.
        His "Agreement with Sir Charles Sedley,"
which ends with 'the very tone and timbre –
        somewhat louder – of a man,' is fucking tight
            enough to make me
think that he must be from here in The Bronx.
This justifies me in naming my essay
        after Sedley's "Baller's Oath"
            like a solo lord.

This sounds realer than "What the Opera Means to Me,"
        and I still demonstrate organization,
            correctness, and substance. I relate
Saul's recognition that God's abandoned him
        to the day when I'll get myself arrested
            or become a janitor
like my third-period teacher says. It's kind
        of freeing, knowing your own name

describes a process of reaching conclusions
>> like the demolition of the Tappan Zee Bridge
>>> when the Mario
Cuomo got built. See, Senator?
Abstentions are for WASPs. We crave attention
>> like that rich boy I hit back
>>> (I forget his name).

I'm not ashamed to tell you, though, that I've no thesis,
>> only the outward form of an argument.
>>> It's as middle-class as I can get.
I don't want 'more for my children.' I want children
>> in folios full, in fresh-pressed with grip strength
>>> like the goddamn Northwest/South Bronx
Region Catholic Schools. I know, Lords Charitable,
>> I've lost the thread about my dad
and this is why Richard Howard was wrong
>> to get me going like we're back in The Bronx.
>>> *Put your pencils down.*
The men I know are prone to disciplining
>> natural speech around strangers,
>>> especially you,

but you should have seen dad when the prosecutors
>> cut him loose, sporting Charlie Croker's glasses
>>> from *The Italian Job*. No – no talking.
Pass your exams forward. We will mail the results…
>> MATTHEW CAREY SALYER STOP WRITING – my father
>>> was always a cliff-hanger, never one
>>>> to bring the house down.
>>> He was only supposed he'd blow the bloody
>>>> doors off with my life.

Cocaine as Trompe L'œil of the Beatific Vision in the Upper East Side

Of the absolute past, I can recall nothing I have
a hunch would return so puckish and peeved
as outlaw me and this nose that didn't break
itself. But now I'm high on the hog, a dog
in a purse: woof, wolf. Brother, I brunch
with the conspicuously fucked who dry-run
Resurrection as midsummer fun, morning dyeing
their gowns for the Eschaton Ball when some, somatic,
eyes bugged like lions from Hick's *Peaceable Kingdom*,
will sway, wanton for lambs, pasture flowers wiping their loins
on my nose, quaint acreage of quaking and command.

*I Regret One of Nine Tattoos Below the Elbow
That Violate the Proper Appearance and Wear of
My Uniform in Accordance with AR-670-1*

I prefer my father the bird to the wonder
mare and dragon strangled in swan

necks (where the bones broke, next
to old mends, I engraved the circuit

of home under paws of their zodiac).
You know how I tried to save everything

but so much of the wreckage was rushed.
Squatters can't be blamed for scars on the mills

or the rash plan of the whole, the lack
of doors and interstates, an interest

in what becomes of a child's map of the soul.
I exfil on the commuter lines, and I, exile,

behave. I ride the peak hour with part-time wives,
finance jocks, and postdocs from candle-houses

with white clapboards. We are encased alive in case
we should cross some carcass yard of freight

where I might exchange this great escape
for the iron house and my chance in the scrap.

III

CONCILIATION WITH AMERICA

He builded the castle
without and within
but he left a wake open
for himself to get in

– Child Ballads 93.E

Argonaut

after Jean-Elmouhoub Amrouche

I moor my fists to the fixed
continents. Bone unspools
its musculature to the crush

of atmosphere and the continents
remain immobile – now what

jut: my head emergent in original night,
its thatched hair ablaze with constellations.
Night owls gaze and shutter the sleeping sand

where my nose is the prow of a struck ship.

Arse Poetica

Lord Randall, I am sick of the sleight, of grace,
still, lifelike as some celebrated deaths, the eel
we split for an hour of middle-school lab.
There is nothing to hunt us

in creation. What I want, I grab (a low criterion
for design), the poem as pietistic stunt or canister
for the dream in which I am always and always
first, forgiven, given

over to nothing awakened, nothing that matters
of life and death can supersede. At the end-all
of appetites, I in mine, you should say thank you
for unlikeliness, its zero,

fain to watch me work up all your nice gods.
But suppose I could parse the ravage from the snare,
the composed pastoral of organic tricks, footed
in our shadows and shadows

of this Great House: its emptiness insists on itself.
I am all I will be at thirtysomething, heavier
but I crawl, brother, doglike on fours to clear its floor.
Christ our caliper,

here is space again, the time being
a thing that is plumb and singular in what I have built.

Lords of Inwood

At The Irish Brigade with the wolfhound banner, *bitch*,
you say, *can keep the house in Queens and go to hell.*
I imagine all that grass to crop for what and flinch –
a bitch it is, but you could just as well

have stayed. Recall us as boys in the lot
on Broadway, stick-fighting: two equable
duelists like the famous brave. Beyond our plot,
a pocked man painted his bodega front with the full

adrenal spectrum of a separate continent. Lambkin,
ours was death's. The landlord of standalone houses
came wearing a summer hat and machete and rent
tall grass from the earth like a ragpicker while, roused,

crackheads swayed like knotweed in the lost foundations.
Now abdicating, specter, weren't we strong then, son?

The Cloisters

Mother's her heart: its pinion the narwhal's tracked

tusk atop the last free hill in Manhattan, and

don't docents hold her cotton breath apart

from the gilt Evangelists, tapestried sequences

of the goring, imported humdrum of regencies

snoring as she dismantles their castle, stone

by stone, unawed by reliefs of the grave

profiles sawn to look alive as eyes awake, alone

in the dark. I'm afraid she is dying. In the dark,

my mother has found her mule to pull the feast

its thousand steps to the house and bones

in a book of hours where the load could break

its forelegs through the clock, the cloister

in the thousand cellars of our day before.

My Father Reading The Sound and the Fury

The flag flapped on bright grass
and a bird. I held

to the fence. *Shut up that moaning,*
Luster said – the bird slants.

I hate Luster and my father
tilts on the edge of the cannonball

bed, turning pages with his shadow-
puppet hand.

First the flag's color and motion
record themselves as

the bird appears – did the bird
tilt the flag or pasture in Benjy's head?

My father's voice rakes scars on his face
into paces of labyrinth.

The nature of Benjy's idiocy subsumes abstractions
such as emotions – their harmonies

taunt and threaten him
as though he is in a theater watching a film

of his life (does his head tilt the flag
or pasture to the bird?)

for this reason
he does not record his present howl.

Time to him it is just a feel for things.
You were asking about my father.

Brooklyn in Postcards of Soviet Russian Fairy-Tales

                I.

Waits at the Q near fare control and the token booth
is a box of snow in Frost Father's bloody-blue coat.

Grandmother, tell me a long word for love so my Father can
die on the quilt of your tongue – will you or won't you?

                II.

Three boats at Broad Channel curled in the afterward peacefully
broken. So Ivan Tsarevich dreamed on the Mohul-bird bridges

across silk grass and steel-flowering sky for three years then fell.
'Over there,' said his bird, 'is the white-stone palace where Wondrous

Beauty lives.' Who knew the wave's white beak, the sign for 'fell'.
Upraised, as in benediction, her bareback bent like a horse-headed prow.

III.

We passed the boardwalk, you on the throat-baring filly, your veil
a crown on a widow's braid. For a silver comb, what wouldn't you?

I with the heart-red peacock caged and padlocked. You, the blue
coating of snow. So we were riding to Rockaways, rock-a-bye,

you and I, on Gray Wolf with Mohul-bird strapped to the saddle.
The greatcoat men in the night, my Wolf at a crossroads of stone.

IV.

A warehouse fire that could take a week to die. Grandmother and I
and the waterfront living a snowflake of magnified moon.

Pity, Father, this work, this woodcut where Grandmother's climbing
the grain of tonight and smoke has lowered your voice like Rapunzeling hair.

Key War in A Minor

portrait of an average bloke
with painted toenails trying to paint
ours break

portrait of the average woman drawing
water from the common well for
hours break

portrait of the hour when
2nd Marines ship south to Nimruz.
Melham relieves current commander Helmand province

and must address the Dyncorp event at Kunduz
Atmar reiterated Atmar
said the Colonel told him prestige was in play

make breaks here and here we must break
men slowly of extravagant habits
said the Lords of War

said there are other issues to consider:
portrait of prestige as a flapping red sheet
portrait for a gunman of the muss in meet

Ask the Birds

> *Fortunati ambo! Si quid mea carmina possunt,*
> *nulla dies umquam memori vos eximet aevo.*
> – The Aeneid, Book IX

When the island towers its spearheads over crowds,
and bluebeard gulls knobble their glass beaks,
burlesquing my cumulous accent that does not break,
I am soured on most monuments. The crane men

are building a new mausoleum for the birds
and from its dragnet of testimonies, they articulate
Virgil's "No day shall erase you from the memory of time,"
that fate of Nisus and Euryalus, killers and lovers both.

Let the poet know lusts are accidents like
the heads on the Rutili's bird-legged
javelins where they spin. Trojans, you see
that the tourists have come to be justified,

to brace against iconoclasm or joint apophasis
as the construction zone lathers its monster in clouds
until I swear I sweat a doppelganger when it would be
like another me to spill the gist of *The Aeneid*

to sightseers on Greenwich and West, its churchy
homage to conquering force. Iowans will watch
the cranes sling low on cheek-bone pylons whipping
high-rises like hobby horse manes, and I ride to

Harlem returning from a little hush war.
Its distance is archaeological as rain

beats storefront light on the Metro
windows into filmstock and the bright

West African dresses of women under the El
drench and sag like slack-necked poppies.
I have not showered in 5,988 miles, not since
I slept on an enormous nerve of the Euphrates,

but my doppelganger's been riding the 1 with Iowans,
watching dusk spill psoriasis on the City's birds,
and wondering as they recall how Hector
held his son above the battlements to lie.

Indeed, I suspect that Virgil knew so much
of political war is a matter of packing clothes
and so much erases us in time's migration
for the birds' sake. One can only hope.

Northern Passage

He carpentered elaborate stairs before
the War, how he survived the War

my grandmother said in her English.
Their Lithuania was something unspoken, kind

of a burdensome luck that stunk
in his foreman house, the one with inch pipes

taken from the warehouse floor at Chase Brass,
with its influence and aurora, the spell

of witch bottles and oak in the small, real yard.
There were mites in the rafters

and I killed one exquisitely because.
True fools,

we scraped the ceiling to haint blue
in the spirit ward,

got back to the neverend.
Like his three-handed Saint Casimir,

say something about the burden of grace,
cracking the beautiful feet of the stairs.

Our Late Departure

*On Reading a Transcript of WNYC's Account of
Senator Robert Fitzgerald Kennedy's Funeral Train*

Opens with tone [   ] a machine-
    generated transcript, the text
        unformatted and prone
to errors in the description. I mean
    fuck's the word '*orkut*' in '*orkut*
        a half-are late, then slowed more when'
            – when what – dumb luck, 'some guys got
killed at Newark, waiting
    for our train as it shot south: their heads
        hang-doggy, mouths shut,' crossing
themselves, and 'one, two, leaned too far, fell'
    flat on the tracks 'four the northbound
        could stop. An at fact, combine wit
            our late departure,'

accounted for crowds in the cooler
    Potomac dusk, the sheer number of strangers
        who'd allowed the kilned, combed
afternoon to pass through their flesh like abstract landscape
    on earthware, a frieze of republican myths
        that might've detailed the Founding of Rome with
            still-life urn-carriers
infilling bogs. Bugs me how 'always some guys
    inna ditch' as my grandpa would've said,
        his had-not like the lot
he'd bought for the Great House, a grandstanding thing
    (come close as he could to rich by '68),

        the planned cornerstone for his capitol skull
            where he'd love the 'little

platoon' (as Edmund Burke called family),
        that 'germ as it were of publick
            affections,' and 'first link
in a series by which we proceed'
        to the common good: good, think,
        Lord Wearie, the men you Great Men
            propose in public
speeches are in the future
        tense. No wonder your world's a mess
            and won't screech to a halt.
That's no way to stress the real grievance
        of crowds in the Late Republic.
        You ought to depict that northbound
            train among the passed-

over, for whom our overwrought
        narrative of change seems like transcripts of chance,
            reformatted and prone
to error in ascribing cause. Consider how, though
        corporate, the roughed-out urn-carriers in your
        frieze of the Fall of the Roman Republic
            remain uncommon
to each other in the late crowd,
        each at their inmost a Great House
            that's crass, immoderate
next to Newark Penn Station's neoclassical forms,
        but apt for the ambitious ostentation
        with which lives of the mind dispute in common
            quorums of our best-

    remembered ghosts. Lord Wearie,
          a Great Man is someone, a ghost is someone
                more construed by the state-
craft of love for our sake, and for all its hardihood
        the death of one man ends
              the communion of spirits within him.
Lords Temporal, when you reclaim the Great House
        it will feel as though you have
watched the birth of a new nation, and it will be
because I'll have forgiven you for what comes
        next: repeat me like the man I am
              innermost inna ditch
        urn-carried from the late departure.

Before Marriage

Doubt will shuttle me under the House of Love,
its draped furniture, parlors for conversation
pieces, our dowries arrayed like perfect dioramas
of settled wars, the still halls where minute maids
knickknack light with their gloves. Doubt will
watch me close through the end as often I've kept
my daughter asleep on the A-train, wiping snack
from her chin, brushing her dream-world, thinking
so, this is the sound of you.

Virgil Explains Limbo to Dante

                    Midlife,
ravenous in the jet wood, wore on his
poet's whet claw; he harrowed the dreck to see
some go, some not; moved on, following me
to a more lexical understanding of place
in the progress of love, our gross recessionals
of the exhausted halfhearted, hoarse to refuge
but choked and fed by his umbilical world.
Expatriation made his metric, home bound
mine: he saw the she-wolf cool in the puddled sun,
tacit but not diabolical, snoozing in forms
without hope, cardio-cartographic, then said
'familiar consultant,' but I had been giving
etymologies: 'LIMBO: Latin, *limbus*, meaning
a hem between sclera and cornea, blood and stem
cells; along the fossa, the margin of the human
heart at the remains of the fetal aperture;
hell's edge, vestibule. It's like the last time
you came home to that prewar apartment: rush hour,
down the block, four flights high, you see the lights
in bedroom windows, hear your children's quarrel
curdle and the kitchen sounds of someone soul
dancing with herself; when she buzzes you in,
you wonder if she will notice that you're drunk
when she's pregnant; your hand is still in line
with the lock in the foyer – but wait, why
turn away? Haven't I taught you a beautiful word?'

Incomplete Self-Portrait as the Last Words of Saints

Blood beloved you call
me I come and adore
this body anywhere
and take no trouble do
you depart: if I ask
you one thing leave me
naked your will be done
at the altar of God
remember one thing
I have seen the most
wonderful things
I forgive the most
wonderful things
(I am trying my best
for interior silence).
I was born poor
I have lived
poor I wish to die
poor things
I adore I commend
this body anywhere
therefore I die
in exile not being
able to suffer
this body anywhere
and take no trouble
over your kingdom come
children depart
I am your will be done
and one more thing
I ask me at the altar

(I am trying my best
for interior silence):
lay this body anywhere
and take no trouble take
the power of blood
your will your servant who hated
iniquity hated righteousness
hated immortal life hated
the cross to loosen me
poor born to die hated
you on the point
of beginning to meet
I will want you
to turn me over
I'm done on this side
I will permit them
blood beloved
Lord receive me
hanging: I am trying
my best to cross.

Wild Colonial Boy

O your lambkin, your long-lost, your farthing dears
    gone, and their rolling-line mill in its snap-
        back ghetto still, shut, pent as the hand
            gestures in grandfather's prim print
                of the Sacred Heart, or his

            song for the half-ten to Queens-
        town, then freighter to trope, his thumb
    on the grind – I'd hazard whoever
built the brass plant, some narrow patrician,
had Dickensian forethought for has-been, who

we are for each other, mother: mother,
    for dears, I'll send back sparrows as blessings
        honed like the visible shrapnel of breath.
            I had no real intention, you
                have to remember, of ever coming home.

Notes & Sources

p. 11 (*inter alia*), **Lambkin:** Ballads about Lambkin, often referred to as 'False,' 'Cruel,' 'Long,' or 'Bold,' appear with numerous variations in Scotland, England, and the United States. In most of these ballads, Lambkin is a skilled mason, hired by Lord Wearie to build him a castle. When Lord Wearie cheats him out of his fee, Lambkin enters his castle, often with the help of an unfaithful housemaid, and exacts a gruesome revenge. The title of Robert Lowell's first book, *Lord Weary's Castle*, alludes to the tale. Versions of the ballad referenced here are taken from Francis Child's *The English and Scottish Popular Ballads* (1882-1898).

p. 14, **an epigram of St. Thomas More:** The poem that inspired "All the Youngbloods" is entitled "Fable of the Sick Fox and the Lion" and appears as #180 in More's *Latin Poems* (*Complete Works* vol. 3.2). The source is an epigrammatic fable, rather than a more conventional epigram associated with Herrick, Johnson, and others, but the dialogue between the lion and the fox aligns More's poem with his stricter examples of the form, many of which plunge the animal kingdom into social violence reserved to the human species.

p. 15, **An tImleach Mór:** Emlaghmore, on the Iveragh Peninsula, Co. Kerry, Ireland.

p. 17, **therefore never built at all and therefore built forever:** In Tennyson's *Idylls of the King*, Bellicent, the Queen of Lothian, tries to dissuade her son, Gareth, from becoming a knight by sending him to work as a kitchen scullion at Camelot. When Gareth first catches a glimpse of Arthur's city, he and his companions are awestruck and incredulous. 'It is enchanted,' Merlin explains, 'for there is nothing in it as it seems / Saving the King' – a city of ideas, ideals, visions, such poetic fabric that 'the city is built / To music, therefore never built at all, / And therefore built forever.' The reference to Mordred's shield is also taken from Tennyson's *Idylls*, which describes it as being 'blank as death.'

p. 18, **"My Heart Leaps Up When I Behold":** Wordsworth's poem, written contemporaneously with "The Cukoo" at Dove Cottage, appears in *Poems, in Two Volumes* (1807). It serves as a sort of *précis* for *Ode: Intimations of Immortality*, which Wordsworth began the day following the composition of these two shorter lyrics. Wordsworth, of course, had a proper middle-class aversion to city-dwelling, as well as a middle-class poet's idea that the speech, thoughts, and lives of 'common men' are characterized by transparent simplicities. Other lines in "Behold, Be Held" thus allude to his "Preface" to *Lyrical Ballads* (1800), as well as "Written in London. September, 1802," in which the unfortunate speaker is 'opprest, / To think that now our life is only drest / For show; mean handy-work of craftsmen, cook, / Or groom!'

p. 29, **Domesday**: Sources for descriptions of the Domesday Book and dialogue in "Department of Social Services" include Richard FitzNeal's *Dialogus de Scaccario* (c. 1179) and the *Anglo-Saxon Chronicle*.

p. 34, **hygge**: The Old Norse etymologies of this term connect it to both thoughtfulness (*hyggja*) and comfort (*hygga*). *Hygge* expresses a Danish cultural idea of middle-class pleasantness, along with associated cultural practices.

p. 35, **Richard's cork leg**: Alludes to the title of Brendan Behan's final, unfinished play. The Chicago theater-going critic Patrick Clinton gives *Richard's Cork Leg* a fair read when he calls it a 'shapeless, plotless, ill-proportioned mass of ghastly puns, music-hall bits, song parodies, speechifying, and heavy-handed satire.'

p. 49, **the fragments of feet / in the slippers**: Raoul Salan's description of the aftermath of an FLN bombing at the Casino de la Corniche, Algiers, 1957, quoted in Alistair Horne's *A Savage War of Peace*. The bomb was detonated during a well-attended performance by Luck Starways and his orchestra. As Horne remarks, the bombing resulted in 'nine dead and eighty-five wounded, nearly half of them women, and many of them having lost legs as a result of the level at which the bomb had exploded.' The anecdotal report of a UFO encounter during the Algerian War is credited to 'Legionnaire N.G.' stationed at Bouhamama during March, 1958.

p. 51, **"The Children of Lir"**: An Irish legend pertaining to the Tuatha Dé Danaan. The earliest versions of the tale occur in MS Egerton 164, held in the British Library, and MS EV vi 4 at the Royal Irish Academy. Like "The Fate of the Children of Uisnigh," "The Fate of the Children of Tuireann," and "The Three Sorrowful Tales of Erin," this is likely a Connacht tale.

p. 53, **a theatrical stage affixed to Europe**: This and linked quotations are taken from Edward Said's *Orientalism: Western Conceptions of the Orient*. Isma'il Pasha was the Khedive of Egypt and Sudan beginning in 1863. A reform-minded modernizer, Isma'il hired employed several American officers after the Civil War to train and advise his armies. After a costly war with Ethiopia, the opening of the Suez Canal, and the accrual of massive foreign debts, Isma'il was deposed by the United Kingdom in 1879.

p. 59, **the very tone and timbre – somewhat louder – than a man**: Lines from Richard Howard's "Agreement with Sir Charles Sedley," first published in *Poetry* (January, 1956). A notorious seventeenth-century rake, Sedley's "Baller's Oath" celebrated his profligate life and contemporaries. Samuel Pepys reports the Lord Chief Justice as claiming that Sedley's ilk caused 'God's judgment and anger [to] hang over us.'

p. 62, **AR-670-1:** This Army manual describes grooming and uniform standards for soldiers. *Section 3-3. Tattoo, Branding, and Body Mutilation Policy* states that: 'Soldiers may have no more than four visible tattoos below the elbow (to the wrist bone) or below the knee. The tattoos in these areas must be smaller than the size of the wearer's hand with fingers extended and joined with the thumb touching the base of the index finger. The total count of all tattoos in these areas may not exceed a total of four.'

p. 70, **Shut up that moaning:** this phrase of Luster's, as well as the scene described in the poem, occurs in Benji's section of William Faulkner's *The Sound and the Fury*. In Benji's consciousness, time takes on the character of what Erich Auerbach calls the 'continuous present' of epic literature, a perspective in which all experiences of the past and present, both psychologically and physically, are 'scrupulously externalized, and narrated in a leisurely fashion.'

p. 72, **Ivan Tsarevich dreamed on the Mohul-bird:** Ivan Tsarevich is a 'placeholder' hero in many Russian fairy tales. The Soviet postcards referenced in this poem depict scenes from "Tsarevich Ivan, the Firebird, and Gray Wolf," collected in Alexander Afanasyev's *Russian Fairy Tales* (1855-1863).

p. 74, **the DynCorp event at Kunduz:** Redacted.

p. 77, **haint blue:** This refers to a light shade of blue made from crushed indigo plants. In the American South, porch roofs, as well as door and window jambs, were often painted haint blue by the Gullah, for whom 'haint' also denoted 'haunt' blue, as the color was believed to repel spirits from entering a home through doorways and windows.

p. 75, **Fortunati ambo! Si quid mea carmina possunt / nulla dies umquam memori vosexime aevo:** These lines from Virgil's *Aeneid*, commemorating the death of a pair of Trojan warriors, are inscribed at the 9/11 Memorial, NYC.

p. 78, **WYNC's account of RFK's funeral train:** NYC Municipal Archives, WNYC Collection, ID T4901. The transcript includes the work of various reporters, including Bill Greenwood, Jim Russell, and Art MacAloon.

p. 79, **germ as it were of publick affections:** These lines are taken from Edmund Burke's *Reflections on the Revolution in France*.

p. 83, **Last Words of Saints:** This poem draws on the reported last words of St. Catherine of Sienna, St. Monica, St. Augustine of Hippo, St. Dominic Savio, Pope St. Pius X, and St. Lawrence.

Acknowledgements

I want to acknowledge journals in which versions of these poems have appeared: *Narrative, Poetry Northwest, The Common, Thrush, The Scores, Charles River Journal, Hunger Mountain, The Adirondack Review, New Madrid, Soundings East, New Orleans Review, Clarion* and *Beloit Poetry Journal*.

I am grateful to Patrick James Errington, William Brewer, Ellen Adair, and John Hennessy for reading this book in manuscript form and providing kind public comments regarding its merit. I am also grateful to Zachary Bos of Pen & Anvil for his careful, attentive design and support throughout the publishing process.

I am also thankful for the friendship of Melissa Green and Richard Howard, who inspire delight in craft and who craft delight.

This book would not exist, nor would I write at all, without Meghan Maguire Dahn.

About the Author

Matthew Carey Salyer is a two-time finalist for the *Iowa Review* Prize in Poetry, a Pushcart nominee, and a semi-finalist for the Brittingham and Felix Pollak Prizes in Poetry. His poems, essays, and fiction have appeared in journals including *Narrative, Massachusetts Review, Hunger Mountain, Poetry Northwest, New Orleans Review, The Common, The Florida Review, Plume,* and *Thrush.* He has published critical essays with *Nineteenth-Century Studies, American Indian Culture and Research Journal, Modern War Institute, Mississippi Quarterly, Studies in Burke and His Time,* and many others. He has taught humanities at the University of Connecticut, Bard College, the United States Coast Guard Academy, and other colleges.

At present, he is an Associate Professor at West Point. He lives in New York City and is the father of three children—his daughters, Rory and Vivian, and his son, Éamon—next to whom all things in this world pale.

Other Titles from Pen & Anvil

Collections
Curtain Speech by Ellen Adair
Saint Medusa by Peter Caputo
Brief Eulogies for Lost Animals by Daniel Hudon
The Garden of Love and Other Stories by David Green
December Poems by Ben Mazer
I Have To Write by Ted Richer
Conscious Explanations by M.A. Schorr
Elgin Pelicans by James Stotts
Uzunburun by Sassan Tabatabai

Chapbooks
Aleppo: Here and Here by James Attor
The Nucleated Vesicle by Jim Colquhoun
Tiles Kissing Close by Nora Delaney
Odysseus & Eden by Cat Dossett
Our Church Is Here by Marcel Inhoff
Moon and Water by Ayla Kutlu
Press Enter to Send by Morgan Racine
Dear Alfredo by Rose Maria Woodson
Against Darkness by Ali Znaidi

Broadsides
Blue Hill Birthday Wishes by Sara Afshar
Jerusalem by Josette Akresh-Gonzales
Cain by Lydia Erickson
Mustang by Abhay K.
New South Wales by Ben Mazer
Alexander Pushkin trans. by Philip Nikolayev
Original Love by April March Penn
Three Poems by David Ferry
The Fall by Arthur Stratusfier Williams

Find a complete list of our publications at
www.penandanvil.com/catalogue

www.ingramcontent.com/pod-product-compliance
Lightning Source LLC
Chambersburg PA
CBHW022118090426
42743CB00008B/909